Lerner SPORTS

ALL-STAR SMACKDOWN

JAMES HARDEN VS. KOBE BRYANT

WHO WOULD WIN?

JOE STANLEY

Lerner Publications ◆ Minneapolis

Lerner Publications Company
An imprint of Lerner Publishing Group, Inc.
241 First Avenue North
Minneapolis, MN 55401 USA

For reading levels and more information, look up this title at www.lernerbooks.com.

Main body text set in Aptifer Sans LT Pro.
Typeface provided by Linotype AG.

Editor: Anne E. Hill

Library of Congress Cataloging-in-Publication Data

Names: Stanley, Joe, 1975– author.
Title: James Harden vs. Kobe Bryant : who would win? / Joe Stanley.
Other titles: James Harden versus Kobe Bryant
Description: Minneapolis, MN : Lerner Publications, [2026] | Series: All-star smackdown (Lerner sports) | Includes bibliographical references and index. | Audience: Ages 7–11 | Audience: Grades 4–6 | Summary: "Kobe Bryant's legendary career included five NBA championships. James Harden is one of the few players in NBA history whose scoring ability could match Bryant's. Can you decide which player was better?"— Provided by publisher.
Identifiers: LCCN 2024043524 (print) | LCCN 2024043525 (ebook) | ISBN 9798765668542 (library binding) | ISBN 9798765683477 (paperback) | ISBN 9798765676097 (epub)
Subjects: LCSH: Guards (Basketball)—United States—Biography—Juvenile literature. | Harden, James, 1989-—Juvenile literature. | Bryant, Kobe, 1978–2020—Juvenile literature. | Basketball players—Rating of—United States—Juvenile literature. | Basketball players—United States—Biography—Juvenile literature. | Basketball—United States—Juvenile literature.
Classification: LCC GV884.A1 S68 2026 (print) | LCC GV884.A1 (ebook) | DDC 796.3230922 [B]—dc23/eng/20241101

LC record available at https://lccn.loc.gov/2024043524
LC ebook record available at https://lccn.loc.gov/2024043525

Manufactured in the United States of America
1-1011548-53822-12/2/2024

TABLE OF CONTENTS

Introduction
Two of the Best 4

Chapter 1
Working for It 8

Chapter 2
Great Moments 14

Chapter 3
Super Scorers 20

Chapter 4
And the Winner Is 24

Smackdown Breakdown. 28
Glossary. 30
Learn More 31
Index 32

Kobe Bryant

INTRODUCTION

TWO OF THE BEST

Los Angeles Lakers superstar Kobe Bryant dribbled the ball beyond the three-point line. He studied the Orlando Magic defenders in front of him. Then Bryant charged toward the basket.

- Kobe Bryant was only the sixth player to join the NBA directly after high school.
- Bryant won five NBA titles.
- In his first three NBA seasons, James Harden started most games on the bench.
- Harden has scored 60 or more points in a game four times.

Magic players closed in on him. Bryant stopped, leaped, and shot the ball. It bounced in for two points. The score gave the Lakers a 95–81 lead.

Bryant and his teammates were playing Game 5 of the 2009 National Basketball Association (NBA) Finals. The Lakers had already won three games in the series. They needed one more win to become NBA champions.

Bryant's two points gave him 30 for the game. The Lakers won 99–86. The victory marked Bryant's fourth NBA championship. It was his first title without former teammate Shaquille O'Neal. Bryant was the team's best player, and he had led the Lakers to the top of the NBA.

James Harden

James Harden has never won the NBA title. But he is one of the greatest scorers in league history. On January 30, 2018, Harden and the Houston Rockets were playing the Orlando Magic. With 45 seconds left in the fourth quarter, Harden made a three-pointer to give his team a 112–107 lead.

The basket gave Harden 59 points in the game. Then he made a free throw to reach 60. Harden finished with 60 points, 10 rebounds, and 11 assists. He became the first NBA player to score at least 60 with a triple-double in the same game.

Bryant and Harden are both all-time great NBA players. But which superstar is better? Let the smackdown begin!

Bryant celebrates on the court after the Lakers won the NBA Finals in June 2009.

Harden launches into the air for a slam dunk during the 2018 NBA playoffs.

CHAPTER 1

Kobe (right) got his love for basketball from his dad, Joe Bryant (left).

WORKING FOR IT

Kobe Bryant's father, Joe Bryant, played eight seasons in the NBA for three different teams. Joe's NBA career ended after the 1982–1983 season. But he wanted to keep playing. In 1984, when Kobe was six, he moved with his family to Italy. Joe Bryant continued playing basketball there.

Kobe and his older sisters, Shaya and Sharia, loved sports. Kobe already played basketball. In Italy, he also began to play soccer. He became a fan of Italian soccer team AC Milan.

Kobe played basketball on junior teams in Italy. He played against kids who were several years older than he was. Kobe was still the best player on the court. He worked hard to improve, often practicing early in the morning while his teammates were still in bed.

Joe Bryant played for the Philadelphia 76ers from 1975 to 1979.

Playing for Lower Merion High School in Pennsylvania, Kobe helped his team win their first state title in 50 years.

In 1992, Kobe's father stopped playing basketball and moved the family back to the US. Kobe was 13 when they arrived in Philadelphia, Pennsylvania. He attended Lower Merion High School.

Kobe played for the varsity basketball team as a first-year student. That season, Lower Merion had a poor 4–20 record. But they soon improved. In the next three seasons, Kobe led the team to a 77–13 record. In his junior season, Kobe won the Pennsylvania Player of the Year award. The next year, he led Lower Merion to its first state title since 1943.

Bryant announced he was entering the NBA draft on April 29, 1996.

Most athletes who hope to play in the NBA go to college after high school. On college teams, they gain experience by competing against great players in arenas packed with fans. But Bryant was special.

On June 26, 1996, the Charlotte Hornets picked him with the 13th overall pick in the NBA draft. Later that day the Hornets traded him to the Lakers. Bryant was the sixth player ever to go from high school straight to the NBA.

CONSIDER THIS

Bryant remained a soccer fan his entire life after his time in Italy. In 2019, Harden became a co-owner of the pro soccer teams Houston Dash and Houston Dynamo.

James Harden was born in 1989 and grew up in Los Angeles, California. His mother, Monja Willis, encouraged her kids to play sports. James has an older sister, Arnique Jelks, and an older brother, Akili Roberson.

James enjoyed watching his brother play high school football. But neither football nor basketball was James's first sport. He liked baseball.

James Harden with his mother, Monja Willis, after receiving his 2017–2018 NBA MVP award

When James was about 10, he played on his first basketball team. He fell in love with the sport. The family hung a hoop on their garage. James practiced and began to develop his shooting style.

James worked hard to improve. At Artesia High School, he often practiced early in the morning before class. During his junior season in 2005–2006, his coach encouraged him to shoot more often. It was good advice. James led Artesia to state titles in 2006 and 2007.

James was a hardworking player during high school.

After high school, Harden went to Arizona State University. He averaged 19 points per game in two college seasons. In 2009, the Oklahoma City Thunder chose him with the third overall pick in the NBA draft. Harden was ready to show that he could compete with the best players in the world.

CHAPTER 2

Bryant dunks the ball during a 2009 game.

GREAT MOMENTS

Bryant was so young when he joined the NBA that he set a record. He started his first game with the Lakers on January 28, 1997. At 18 years and 158 days old, he was the youngest player to ever start an NBA game.

That season, Bryant took part in the NBA Slam Dunk Contest. Fans roared as he leaped and spun to dunk the ball. For one dunk, he jumped, passed the ball between his legs, and then slammed it through the hoop. The high score he received for the move helped make him the youngest dunk champion in NBA history.

In December 2005, the Lakers played the Dallas Mavericks. Bryant scored an amazing 32 points in the first half. He was just getting started. In the third quarter, he scored 30 more points. With the team way ahead, Lakers coach Phil Jackson pulled Bryant out of the game. Bryant's 62 points in three quarters were more than Dallas's entire team had scored.

Bryant takes a jump shot in a 2005 game against the Dallas Mavericks.

Bryant's highest-scoring game came on January 2, 2006. He made shots from all around the court to score 81 points. The Lakers beat the Toronto Raptors 122–104. Bryant's incredible total ranks second in NBA history to Wilt Chamberlain's 100-point game in 1962.

By the 2015–2016 season, age and injuries had slowed Bryant. He averaged 17.6 points per game, one of the lowest averages of his career. His final game with the Lakers came on April 13, 2016. Facing the Utah Jazz, Bryant played like a younger version of himself. He scored 60 points to lead his team to a 101–96 victory.

Bryant takes a shot in a game against the Toronto Raptors in November 2006.

CONSIDER THIS

Bryant scored 60 or more points in a game six times in his NBA career. Harden has done it four times.

James Harden's NBA career got off to a much slower start than Bryant's did. Harden began most games on the bench for the Thunder. In his rookie season, he didn't start any games. In 2010–2011, he started five times. The next season, he started only twice.

Harden leaps to dunk the ball during a 2011 game against the Dallas Mavericks.

In October 2012, the Thunder traded Harden to the Houston Rockets. In Houston, Harden's career took off. He started 78 games in 2012–2013 and averaged almost 26 points per game.

Harden's biggest game so far came in 2018 when he racked up a triple-double against the Magic. His 60 points set a Rockets record for points in a game. But it wasn't the only time that Harden scored 60 or more points. In 2019, he did it three times.

Harden (left) tries to get around Orlando defender Mario Hezonja during a January 2018 game.

Harden (left) is defended by Tim Hardaway Jr. of the New York Knicks in 2019.

On January 23, 2019, Harden scored 61 of his team's 114 points. He helped the Rockets beat the New York Knicks 114–110. Two months later, he did it again. Harden scored 61 points in a 111–105 win against the San Antonio Spurs.

In November 2019, the Rockets faced the Atlanta Hawks. Harden scored from long range and close to the basket. He made eight three-point shots and 20 free throws. His 60 points helped the Rockets destroy the Hawks 158–111.

CHAPTER 3

Bryant (right) attempts to dribble the ball past Dwyane Wade during the 2012 NBA All-Star Game.

SUPER SCORERS

Bryant's personal stats are some of the best in NBA history. In 2005–2006 and 2006–2007, he led the league in points per game. He finished first in the league in total points scored four times.

Fans, players, and NBA reporters voted for Bryant to play in 18 All-Star Games. He won the game's Most Valuable Player (MVP) award four times. In 2007–2008, Bryant averaged 28.3 points per game and led the Lakers to the title. After the season, he won the NBA MVP award.

Personal stats can tell fans a lot about players. But many think that team stats are more important because basketball is a team sport. By that measure, few players can compare to Bryant. He helped the Lakers win five NBA titles. In 2009 and 2010, he won the NBA Finals MVP award.

Bryant (right) holds the NBA MVP trophy in May 2008.

CONSIDER THIS

In 2018, Bryant won an Academy Award for best animated short film for *Dear Basketball.* The movie is based on a poem Bryant wrote in 2015 to announce his retirement from the NBA.

Harden is one of the greatest scorers in NBA history. He's also a fantastic passer. He twice led the league in assists per game, something Bryant didn't do. Some critics of Bryant's play have said that he often didn't share the ball with teammates.

Harden at the 2015 NBA All-Star Game on February 15, 2015

Harden with his 2017–2018 NBA MVP trophy

Harden has been voted to 10 All-Star Games. He led the league in points per game three times. In 2017–2018, he was the NBA MVP. But Harden can't match Bryant's team success. Harden has only reached the NBA Finals once. In 2018, his Thunder lost to the Miami Heat in five games.

CHAPTER 4

Bryant (right) shoots over Harden during a January 2013 game.

AND THE WINNER IS

When choosing a winner of this smackdown, there is no right or wrong answer. Fans have different reasons for choosing their favorite. Bryant and Harden are both all-time great NBA players.

Both players are world-class scorers. They had some of the highest-scoring games and seasons in NBA history. Bryant played stronger defense than Harden, and Harden was better at setting up his teammates to score.

Harden passes the ball during a 2023 game.

One area where Harden can't match Bryant is NBA titles. Only 13 players have won more championships than Bryant's five. Harden is still seeking his first series win in the NBA Finals. That's the reason Bryant comes out on top in this smackdown.

Who is your winner? Do you agree that Bryant's NBA Finals success makes him the smackdown champ? Or does Harden's ability to score and make great passes to his teammates put him over the top? Think it over and make your choice!

Harden looks to make a pass on the court.

Bryant celebrating one of his five NBA championship wins.

SMACKDOWN BREAKDOWN

KOBE BRYANT

Date of birth: August 23, 1978
Height: 6 feet 6 (2 m)
NBA championships: 5
NBA scoring titles: 2
Points per game: 25
Assists per game: 4.7

Statistics are accurate through the 2023–2024 NBA season.

JAMES HARDEN

Date of birth: August 26, 1989
Height: 6 feet 5 (1.9 m)
NBA championships: 0
NBA scoring titles: 3
Points per game: 24.1
Assists per game: 7.1

GLOSSARY

assist: a pass from a teammate that leads directly to a basket

draft: when teams take turns choosing new players

free throw: an open shot taken from behind a set line after a foul by an opponent

rebound: grabbing and controlling the ball after a missed shot

rookie: a first-year player

slam dunk: a shot in basketball made by jumping high into the air and throwing the ball down through the basket

start: to begin the game on the court instead of on the bench

title: championship

triple-double: when a player reaches at least 10 in three different stats in a game

varsity: the top team at a school

LEARN MORE

Kiddle: National Basketball Association Facts for Kids
https://kids.kiddle.co/National_Basketball_Association

Kjartansson, Kjartan Atli. *Legends of the NBA*. New York: Abbeville Kids, 2022.

Moussavi, Sam. *Houston Rockets*. New York: Lightbox Learning, 2023.

Naismith Memorial Basketball Hall of Fame: Kobe Bryant
https://www.hoophall.com/hall-of-famers/kobe-bryant/

NBA: James Harden
https://www.nba.com/player/201935/james-harden

Stewart, Audrey. *G.O.A.T. Basketball Shooting Guards*. Minneapolis: Lerner Publications, 2025.

INDEX

Arizona State University, 13
Atlanta Hawks, 19

Bryant, Joe, 8

Chamberlain, Wilt, 16
Charlotte Hornets, 11

Dallas Mavericks, 15

Houston Rockets, 6, 18–19

Jackson, Phil, 15

Los Angeles, CA, 12
Los Angeles Lakers, 4–5, 11, 14–16, 20–21

NBA Finals, 5, 21, 23, 26

Oklahoma City Thunder, 13, 17–18, 23
O'Neal, Shaquille, 5
Orlando Magic, 4–6, 18

Philadelphia, PA, 10

San Antonio Spurs, 19

Toronto Raptors, 16

Utah Jazz, 16

Willis, Monja, 12

PHOTO ACKNOWLEDGMENTS

Image credits: Jeff Gross/Getty Images, p. 4; Bob Levey/Getty Images, pp. 5, 18; Ronald Martinez/Getty Images, pp. 6, 7, 20; Noel Vasquez/Getty Images, p. 8; Focus on Sport/Getty Images, p. 9; Pete Bannan/MediaNews Group/Main Line Media News via Getty Images, p. 10; Rusty Kennedy/AP Photo, p. 11; Allen Berezovsky/Getty Images, p. 12; Bob Leverone/Sporting News via Getty Images via Getty Images, p. 13; Jed Jacobsohn/Getty Images, p. 14; Robert Laberge/Getty Images, p. 15; John W. McDonough/Sports Illustrated via Getty Images, pp. 16, 27; Christian Petersen/Getty Images, p. 17; Elsa/Getty Images, p. 19; Armando Arorizo/Bloomberg via Getty Images, p. 21; Jim McIsaac/Getty Images, p. 22; Joe Scarnici/Getty Images for Turner Sports, p. 23; Scott Halleran/Getty Images, pp. 24, 26; Meg Oliphant/Getty Images, p. 25; Ethan Miller/Getty Images, p. 28; Jonathan Daniel/Getty Images, p. 29.

Cover images: Ringo Chiu/Xinhua via Alamy (Harden); AP Photo/Jeff Chiu (Bryant).